ESL Reading Activities for Teenagers and Adults:

Practical Ideas for the Classroom

Jackie Bolen

(www.eslactivity.org)

Table of Contents

About the Author: Jackie Bolen

I taught English in South Korea for a decade to every level and type of student. I've taught every age from kindergarten kids to adults. Most of my time centered around teaching at two universities: five years at a science and engineering school out in the rice paddies of Chungcheongnam-Do, and four years at a major university in Busan where I taught high level classes for students majoring in English. I now teach ESL/EFL students in Vancouver, Canada. In my spare time, you can usually find me outside surfing, biking, hiking, or on the hunt for the most delicious kimchi I can find. It's not so easy in Vancouver!

In case you were wondering what my academic qualifications are, I hold a Master of Arts Degree in Psychology. During my time in Korea I successfully completed both the Cambridge CELTA and DELTA certification programs. With the combination of ten years teaching ESL/EFL learners of all ages and levels, and the more formal teaching qualifications I obtained, I have a solid foundation on which to offer teaching advice. I truly hope that you find this book useful and would love it if you sent me an email with any questions or feedback that you might have.

How did I get into teaching English reading? Well, I kind of fell into it when I moved from teaching young kids to university students. I taught ESL reading to beginners where we focused on learning how to read and the ABC's. I also taught far more advanced students the ins and outs of reading for academic purposes. There's also been a fair share of helping students prepare for popular English proficiency exams like the TOEFL or TOEIC.

With time, I found that I liked teaching reading far more than I did conversation and speaking. As a result, I requested more of these classes from the administration at my university and they happily complied. Many teachers don't like to teach reading classes because they perceive them as a little bit boring. However, I always found it a nice change of pace and couldn't get enough of them.

The activities and games in this book are ones that I've used in my own classes and are tried and true! If you only teach beginners, there are also lots of activities for you. It really is a book for anyone who teaches ESL/EFL reading.

Jackie Bolen around the Internet

ESL Speaking (www.eslactivity.org)

Jackie Bolen (www.jackiebolen.com)

Twitter: @bolen_jackie

Email: jb.business.online@gmail.com

You may also want to check out some of other books on Amazon (search for Jackie Bolen), but here are a few of my most popular titles:

39 No-Prep/Low-Prep ESL Speaking Activities

39 Awesome 1-1 ESL Activities

101 ESL Activities for Teenagers and Adults

Life After ESL: Foreign Teachers Returning Home

Top 10 Tips for Teaching ESL Reading

#1: It's Not Just About Reading for Detail

It's easy to focus most of our reading activities on reading for detail. By that, I mean that our students read a text and then answer some comprehension questions. However, there's a lot more to it and there are a huge range of reading sub-skills to consider working on. For example:

- Skimming

- Scanning

- Inferring meaning

- Summarizing

The next section of this book has more details about reading sub-skills and the activities in this book are designed to practice a variety of them.

#2: Don't Forget to Set the Context

In any lesson that we teach, reading included, it's key to set the context before jumping into the lesson. This helps to prime students for what they're about to learn or in this case, read. It's possible to do this in any number of ways, but perhaps the simplest way to do it is to get students to talk with a partner about the topic of the reading. You could also consider showing a short video, or having students look at a related picture.

#3: Consider Students' Needs

In terms of needs for our students when it comes to reading, there are obviously some very different ones. Compare for example someone who wants to improve their reading skills to make reading menus in restaurants when traveling easier to someone who wants to understand complicated scientific journals. Of course, improving reading skills for English proficiency tests is another major reason why students may be in our class.

If you're not sure what kinds of needs your students have, ask them! Then, do your best to tailor your lessons to their specific situations. I generally try to focus some class time to general reading skills and then some time to the specific reading needs of the students.

#4: Vocabulary is Important

If you've ever studied another language, maybe you've had the experience of understanding almost nothing of what you read because your vocabulary was quite limited. We've all been there and it's certainly a stressful experience.

If your students are quite weak when it comes to vocabulary, then you'll have to be especially careful at selecting reading passages. They should be challenging to our students but not so challenging that they're overwhelming. Of course, they can also be useful tools for learning new vocabulary so consider pre-teaching some words that you think your students may not be familiar with before getting started.

#5: Use a Variety of Comprehension Questions

When it comes to comprehension questions, I like to mix things up a little bit and keep my students on their toes! This means a wide variety of question styles such as:

- true/false

- multiple choice

- open-ended questions

- short answer questions

- summarize the main idea

- order events in the story

- identifying genre structure, e.g. climax of story, or thesis sentence in an essay

- opinion questions

In general, I'll have students answer the questions on their own, then compare with a partner and finally we'll check them as a class. However, if your students are focusing on reading skills for a specific English proficiency exam, then the majority of the questions should be similar in style so that they can do some targeted practice.

#6: Does it Apply to Real-Life?

I find that the best reading lessons are those that can apply to real life. This means choosing topics and texts carefully. Hopefully our students can learn some new things as well as improve their reading skills! Or, think to themselves, "That's how I feel a lot too!," or, "My experience is the same as that person." When students have these kinds of moments, the lesson will be far more memorable which will go a long way towards improving skills.

#7: Sneak in Some Pronunciation

During my years of teaching, I've run across some students with very impressive vocabulary and reading skills. Except when they spoke or read out loud, I discovered that they had terrible pronunciation! It always surprises me, but it's certainly a real thing that can happen with some students who mostly study on their own without a conversation partner or teacher.

It's for this reason that I like to include some pronunciation work in my lessons of the particularly difficult words. Another option is to have students read out loud, either in class or as a homework assignment (it can be recorded as a *YouTube* video or audio recording).

#8: Use Authentic Materials for Higher-Level Students

For students who are at a high-intermediate or advanced level, it can be very motivating to use authentic materials. By authentic materials, I mean things like restaurant menus, newspapers and magazines, travel brochures, etc. that are designed for English speakers and not for ESL/EFL students. These can often be far more interesting than what you'd find in a textbook and are a nice change of pace for our students.

#9: Teach Reading Strategies

The reading strategies to teach depend heavily on the genre of writing. However, some things to consider teaching are:

- Finding the thesis statement and topic sentences

- Checking for transitional words or phrases

- Reading the first and last sentences of each paragraph first

- Circling key vocabulary words

- Taking notes in the margins about main points

- Reading the comprehension questions first whenever possible

#10: Work on Improving Other English Skills

The best way to improve English skills, or any language skills for that matter is a balanced approach. Even if students want to focus on improving their reading, I'll generally plan balanced lessons that have a bit of speaking, listening, reading and writing, along with vocabulary and grammar. However, a reading text will likely be at the center of the lesson. It's also important to do accuracy as well as fluency elements. All too often teachers focus on accuracy and teach-to-the-test at the expense of fluency.

What are the Reading Sub-Skills?

When planning a reading lesson, it's useful to keep the following sub-skills in mind and each activity should focus on at least one of these things. Here's a brief overview of the main reading sub-skills.

Reading Fluency

When reading something in a language that's not our first one, it's easy to get bogged down trying to understand every single word. This usually comes at the expense of reading fluency. Fluency is important though, not just in speaking but in reading as well. After all, nobody wants an employee who takes two hours to understand a report in English that should have taken 20 minutes to figure out.

Scanning

We often have to scan or look for specific facts in a text. There are a countless examples of this, but here are just a few of the things that we very quickly look for in a text:

- Numbers

- Times and dates

- Proper nouns

- A certain part of speech

- Key words

- Transition signals

- Opinion phrases (I think . . .)

- Etc.

The key thing is that this should happen very quickly and if we allow our students too much time to do these tasks, it mostly defeats the purpose of it as it becomes more about reading for detail (see below).

Skimming

Skimming is similar to scanning but the key difference is that it's reading rapidly to gain a general overview of something, instead of looking for something specific. A nice way to help our students with this is to give them some simple true/false questions about a text and then a very limited amount of time for a quick first read-through. After that, they can answer the questions and then have more time for a detailed reading. Or, instruct students to only read the first sentence of each paragraph in the text. Explain that topic sentences often give enough information about each paragraph to provide the main idea of the entire text.

Reading for Detail

There are many times when we have to read something thoroughly and in detail in order to understand the finer points of it. This is probably the reading sub-skill that most English teachers are very familiar with. Students can underline or circle facts, dates, names, etc., so that if they're doing a reading test they can go back afterwards to easily find the question's answer or if writing an essay find quotes to support their thesis.

Predicting

Prediction is a key skill for both listening and reading. The reason for this is that if we can predict what's coming, we'll likely be able to understand it more deeply and easily. One simple way to help our students with this is to show them a headline and then have them predict some things about it. For example, what questions will be answered in the reading, some key vocabulary words they might hear, or a general overview of what the reading might be about.

Recognizing Links/Understanding Discourse Markers

All texts are organized in some fashion and have various discourse markers (aka transition signals) throughout. The purpose of a discourse marker is to organize a text into segments or sections. One simple example is in a lecture where the speaker might use, "First, second, third, finally."

In addition, most texts have links between sections and sentences to assist with understanding. One simple example is the following: "JOHN came home late last night. HE . . ." Or, formal essays often have a transition sentence to link paragraphs together and they'll also have a sentence in the conclusion that restates the thesis statement from the introduction.

Infer Meaning from Context/Guessing the Meaning of Unknown Words

When reading, there are often words that we don't know, even when reading in our first language. This is the same experience that our students have when reading something in English. However, by understanding the context, either the bigger picture of the entire text, or the smaller picture of the surrounding words, we can often guess what the word we don't know means. This allows for far more fluent reading!

If a student asks me what a certain word means, I'll ALWAYS get them to make a guess first. They're often right!

Proofreading/Editing

Proofreading and editing are vital skills for the writing process. They are also considered to be reading sub-skills because they are essentially a very close reading of a text in order to look for errors.

Inferring Attitude/Feeling/Meaning

Most things that we read, particularly fiction or things like advice columns have attitudes, feelings or meanings behind the words. Understanding how they are can influence the reading of the text can also assist with understanding the bigger picture.

Note Taking

Note taking is a writing sub-skill that can either be done with listening as in the case of a lecture, or through reading as in the case of a report. It's a skill that most English learners struggle with because it requires identifying only the key or main points of the text.

Reading Out Loud

Although some students may be fluent when it comes to reading inside their head, they may struggle with pronunciation and reading out loud. We can help them out with this skill by giving them some practice in class.

Identifying Words or Grammatical Constructions

The most basic reading sub-skill is understanding words and grammatical constructions. This is often where beginners are at as things like note-taking, inferring attitudes, or recognizing discourse markers are too complex for them in most cases.

Identifying the Text Type/Purpose/Organization

Every text is written for a reason. Identifying this reason, along with the kind of text it is and the basic organizational structure can greatly assist with understanding it.

ESL Reading Activities for All Levels

An Irrelevant Sentence

Skill: Reading

Reading Sub-Skills: Reading for detail, recognizing links, identifying the text type

Time: 5-20 minutes

Level: Beginner-advanced

Materials Required: Texts with one irrelevant sentence

A key reading sub-skill is the ability to understand the text type and organization of it. For example, an email clearly has a different organizational style than a novel would. This activity is designed to help our students recognize things that seem out of place when considering the text type. This requires both reading for detail and recognizing links between parts of a text.

The way it works is that the teacher prepares one, or more than one reading texts, inserting an irrelevant sentence into each one. How obvious to make it depends on the level of the students. Students have to use their reading for details skills to find which sentence doesn't belong.

Procedure:

1. Prepare some reading texts with one irrelevant sentence in each one.

2. Students read each one and choose the rogue sentence.

3. Discuss as a class why it doesn't fit.

Brochure Scanning

Skill: Reading

Reading Sub-Skill: Scanning

Time: 10-20 minutes

Level: Beginner-advanced

Materials Required: Travel brochures

Scanning is reading for specific information and it makes an excellent ESL reading activity. Language learners tend to focus on trying to understand every word, so they need to practice quickly finding specific key words. This will increase their reading speed in general and help move them towards more natural reading practices.

To provide realistic practice, collect travel brochures, bus timetables and menus. If you do not have local access to any of these, a quick Google search will give you a wide variety. Here are a few sample scenarios to use, depending on the level of your student.

Option #1: Intermediate-Advanced Students

Find a vacation bargain. Give students a budget, length of travel, and any other limitations, such as "type" of holiday (beach, historical, adventure, etc.). This is highly variable according to the materials you have available and student levels.

The students should scan the brochure for trips that match the criteria. To add more speaking, begin by discussing the students' ideas of a great vacation, and then work together to find a trip that matches those criteria.

Option #2: High Beginner Students

Try a new restaurant. Have students find menu items with certain qualities, such as vegetarian, lamb, or no onions. Can he/she make a reservation for 8PM on Monday? What is the phone number for reservations? And so on.

Option #3: Beginner Students

Take a bus from point A to point B for a meeting at a given time and then return. Have students use a bus timetable to plan the journey. Have them quickly scan the brochure to find the requested information.

Teaching Tips:

For lower level students, have printed questions for them to use with the brochure. For example, "What time is the last bus to _____ on Sunday nights?"

If you are looking online for printable realia, add "PDF" to your search and the results will begin with PDF files that match your search terms.

Or, if you can get a Flight Centre or Thomson brochure, you can get a lot of mileage out of it beyond scanning. They are basically magazines with hundreds of travel packages of all types and for a range of budgets, although nothing is too luxurious. The higher the level, the more freedom you have to expand the activity.

Procedure:

1. In advance, get a brochure or print one from the Internet. Restaurant menus, bus timetables and travel brochures are perfect for this. See the examples above for some ideas.

2. Prepare some questions for students to answer using the information in the brochure.

3. Explain to students that they are not to read word for word. They should only be reading to find the answers to the questions.

4. Have them find answers to the questions.

Proofreading Practice

Skills: Writing/reading

Reading Sub-Skill: Proofreading/editing

Time: 5-10 minutes

Level: Beginner-advanced

Materials Required: Worksheet with errors

The ability to correct errors through proofreading and editing is a very important reading and writing skill. However, there's more to it than just telling our students to find the mistakes! We can actually teach them how to do this in a far more systematic way.

How you design this activity will vary greatly depending on the level of your students. Beginner level students can generally only proofread 1-3 things when they start developing self-editing skills. For example, tell them to check that the first word of each sentence is capitalized and has a period at the end. Advanced level students can handle a wide range of errors that include punctuation, spelling, grammar, vocabulary, flawed logic and more.

Not proofreading writing is the biggest writing mistake. This applies to students who are studying English as a second or third language, as well as native speakers. Here's the advice that I give my students about this important topic.

After you write, allow yourself some time to read your work. If you're doing a writing test that is one hour long, I recommend the following:

1. 5 minutes planning. Write a few notes. Make a plan. What is your first, second, and third main point (if writing an essay)?

2. 45-50 minutes writing.

3. 5-10 minutes proofreading. Check writing for any mistakes. I recommend double-spacing, so it's easy to make any changes if you need to. Cross off what you wrote and then write in the line above it.

Reading out loud each and every word is a good habit to get into. Pay close attention to things like subject-verb agreement (He is, She goes), spelling, capital letters, punctuation, etc.

If students do only one thing to improve their writing, it's this! ALWAYS proofread. Always! Here's a proofreading checklist I made for my university students in South Korea that you may want to consider using with yours: www.jackiebolen.com/proofreading.

Procedure:

1. Explain to your students about proofreading and give them a checklist for things to check.

2. Prepare a worksheet of sentences, a paragraph or an essay (depending on the level) that has some errors from the checklist on it.

3. Students have to go through the worksheet finding the errors. Check answers together as a class.

Running Dictation

Skills: Writing/listening/speaking/reading

Reading Sub-Skills: Reading for detail, recognizing links, understanding discourse markers

Time: 15 minutes

Level: Beginner-advanced

Materials Required: The "dictation" + some way to attach it to the walls or board.

This is one of my favorite activities which covers reading, writing, listening and speaking. In terms of reading sub-skills, it hits a few of them. First is reading for detail as students have to read and then remember each word to tell their partner. Secondly, students have to recognize links and understand discourse markers in order to put their sentences into the correct order to form a cohesive whole.

There are a wide variety of English styles you can choose: poems, song lyrics, a short story, famous quotes—the list is almost limitless. For example, you might make up a story or conversation that is a few sentences long (less than ten). You'll want to include plenty of examples of your intended grammatical point.

Put each sentence on a strip of paper and you can also put another strip of paper on top to prevent cheating. Put these in random order around the classroom in various locations. I make sure to space them out equally so that the game is fair for everyone.

The students will be in teams of two. One person is the reader and one is the writer. The reader gets up, walks to the first location, reads a bit of the passage, returns to their desk, and tells it to the writer. They go back to remember more of it and so on and so on.

At the end, the students have to put the song or conversation in order by numbering their sentences. When they're done, I'll check their writing and if there aren't many mistakes plus the order is correct, that team is the winner. How many mistakes you allow depends on the level of your students.

There are a number of ways to correct the passage. The first is to only check the top couple of teams that may be getting a prize of some kind. The second is to put the original version up on the PowerPoint and have students check their own, although this does rely on honesty if some sort of prize is involved. Finally, each pair can trade papers with another pair and check against the original.

Tell your students before the activity starts that standing at the strip of paper and then yelling to their partner instead of walking over to them is not allowed or they will be disqualified.

Teaching Tip:

Make sure you let your students know what cheating is (yelling, the "reader/speaker" touching the pen, using their phone camera) and if that happens their team will automatically be disqualified.

Procedure:

1. Prepare a simple story or conversation with your target grammar and put each sentence on a strip of paper.

2. Put the papers around the classroom on the wall, equally spaced out.

3. Divide the students into pairs: one writer and one reader.

4. The reader stands up, walks to the station and reads a paper, then goes back to the writer and tells what they read to the writer, who must write it. The reader can go back to a single paper as many times as required.

5. This procedure of reading, speaking, listening, and writing continues until the team has all the sentences down on their paper.

6. The two students put the story or conversation in the correct order.

7. The teacher can check for accuracy and meaning and decide if it's acceptable, or not.

Same Same but Different

Skill: Reading

Reading Sub-Skills: Identifying the key points, note-taking

Time: 5-10 minutes

Level: Beginner-advanced

Materials Required: Text

This is a simple reading activity that requires students to identify the key points of a text and to also work on note taking. In advance, prepare two slightly different versions of a text with a few key things changed.

Students read the first version and take notes. Then, they read another version that has some changes (the amount depends on the length of the passage and level of students) but I usually tell students how many changes I've made before the second reading. Students can take notes about the changes and then compare with a partner. Then, check answers together as a class. Of course, don't allow access to the first version (I collect the original papers or remove it from the PowerPoint). Instead, students have to rely on their notes and their memory.

Procedure:

1. Choose a text.

2. Students read the passage and take notes about the key points. Collect the papers or remove it from the PowerPoint

3. Tell students that they're going to read a slightly different version with some key things that are changed. Let them know how many changes there are.

4. Student read the new version and compare the changes from the original with a partner.

5. Check answers together as a class.

Scanning

Skill: Reading

Reading Sub-Skill: Scanning

Time: 5 minutes

Level: Beginner-advanced

Materials Required: A text

Scanning means to read a text quickly while searching for specific information or facts. This is necessary to do in a number of real life situations, not to mention for English reading proficiency tests. However, without some targeted activities and practice, most students don't naturally do this in another language!

One way to help our students with scanning is to find a short text and then prepare some simple true/false questions. Show the questions to the students first and then give them only a short amount of reading time to find the answers. It is important to stress that they should identify—and circle or underline what the specific number, date, name, etc., is that the answer to the question requires so that they don't read every word and practice the skill of scanning—this is especially important for beginner (doing a brief demonstration is also a good idea) and low intermediate students, and even sometimes for advanced too.

At the end of the reading time, students turn their papers over and try to answer the questions. They can compare with a partner and then together as a class. This scanning activity can lead into a more detailed second reading exercise.

Procedure:

1. Talk about scanning and why it's an important reading skill.

2. Give students some simple true/false questions related to a text.

3. Allow a short amount of time for reading.

4. Students answer the questions and compare with a partner.

5. Check answers together as a class.

Skimming

Skill: Reading

Reading Sub-Skill: Skimming

Time: 5 minutes

Level: High-beginner to advanced

Materials Required: A text

Skimming means to read quickly in order to get a general overview of the information. It's vital that our students are able to do this because we're required to do this in many real-life situations (as well as for academic purposes). For example, it's not common to read a travel brochure word-for-word. Instead, we quickly look through it to get a general idea of what it says in order to make a decision.

One way to help our students do this is to limit how long they can take to do a first quick read-through of a text. First, give students some very basic comprehension questions that aim at the big picture of the text. Allow them some time to read them. Then, give students a very short amount of time for skimming. At the end of the allotted time, students turn the text over and attempt to answer the questions. Finally, they compare answers with a partner and then together as a class.

Teaching Tip:

Absolute beginners who are trying to understand a text word by word will not be able to do this activity effectively so I recommend it only for high-beginners and above. In addition, there is a large variance between what this activity will look like for a high-beginner student and one who is advanced. More advanced students will be able to handle longer and more complicated texts, more difficult questions and a greater number of them.

Procedure:

1. Talk about skimming, why it's necessary and how to do it.

2. Give students some comprehension questions related to a text.

3. Allow students a very short amount of reading time.

4. Students answer the questions and compare with a partner.

5. Check answers together as a class.

Story Re-Creation

Skill: Reading

Reading Sub-Skills: Reading for detail, inferring attitude/feeling, inferring meaning from context

Time: 30+ minutes

Level: High-beginner to advanced

Materials Required: Various short stories

Try out this fun reading activity that works on a variety of sub-skills including reading for detail and inferring attitudes or feeling. Prepare one short story filled with lots of action. Each group should have a different story and the group size depends on the number of characters in each story. Give students some time to read their group's story and prepare to act it out. They are not to speak but only do it with actions.

In advance of each story, show some comprehension questions that you'll ask the class after the group is finished acting. The group acts out the story and then sees if they can answer the comprehension questions. You can elicit some answers and perhaps talk more about the feeling or mood of the story or see if the class was able to understand it based on the acting.

Teaching Tip:

This activity is better for smaller classes of fewer than ten students. This is due to the noise during preparation, time constraints with a typical 1-1.5 hour class, amount of preparation required by the teacher and overall classroom management.

Procedure:

1. Prepare a different story for each group (group size depends on characters in the story).

2. Give some preparation time to read the story and practice acting it out, without words.

3. Before each story, show the class some simple comprehension questions they'll need to answer.

4. The group acts out their story.

5. The class can answer the questions.

6. (Optional): Discuss the story, including feelings, mood, sequence of action, etc.

Story Timeline

Skills: Reading/listening/speaking

Reading Sub-Skills: Understanding discourse markers, recognizing links, identifying the text type

Time: 10-15 minutes

Level: Beginner-advanced

Materials Required: Sentence strips of important events in a novel

Extensive reading is an excellent way to build your students' vocabulary quickly, but you and your students probably don't want to spend too much class time reading novels. One option is to assign a novel for homework and in each lesson, go over unfamiliar vocabulary or situations as well as any number of extension activities. This is one such activity and it can be done individually or in small groups.

In terms of reading sub-skills, an activity like this one can be very useful for a number of reasons. It helps students gain a greater understanding of discourse markers, links between sections of the text and also an awareness of the type of text they're reading.

A timeline, or chronology, of important plot events is a useful way to have the class briefly summarize the story chapter by chapter. A timeline will help them keep track of the story while providing practice determining important events.

Teaching Tips:

For higher-level students, consider adding extra, unimportant plot events and have the students select only the important ones to order.

Penguin has six levels of graded readers that include simplified versions of popular novels and classics that you may want to consider using with your students.

Procedure:

1. In advance, prepare sentence strips describing important events in the plot.

2. Have the students order the sentence strips you have provided. Check answers together.

What are you Watching Tonight?

Skills: Reading/speaking/listening

Reading Sub-Skill: Scanning

Time: 10-15 minutes

Level: High-beginner to advanced

Materials Required: TV guide

Maybe you've had a student complain that what they have to read in ESL/EFL textbooks is too boring! If this is the case, mix it up a little bit and bring some real life into the classroom. Take a look online for a TV schedule or guide and print out enough for the class.

Then, ask students some questions such as what show is playing at a certain time. Or, to choose a show they want to watch at 7pm tonight and tell their partner why. These kinds of questions help students work on their scanning skills as they have to look quickly for very specific information.

Finally, students can take a turn asking a partner some questions. This quick activity can certainly lead into a full lesson on TV, hobbies, TV stars, etc.

Procedure:

1. Find a TV guide online and print off enough copies for the class.

2. Ask students some questions based on it.

3. Students can ask a partner some questions.

ESL Reading Activities for Lower-Level Students

Correction Relay

Skills: Reading/writing

Reading Sub-Skill: Proofreading

Time: 10+ minutes

Level: Beginner-intermediate

Materials Required: Worksheet with errors

This is an activity that uses speed and competition to make something old (error correction) new again. Students of all levels should be quite familiar with finding and correcting errors in sentences. By adding a relay aspect, it will (hopefully) make an important but sometimes tedious skill new and more interesting and of course, working on proofreading is a vital reading skill for our students.

To prepare the activity, create a worksheet with 10-15 errors. You can focus your errors on one aspect of vocabulary, such as synonyms and antonyms, or more simply, misuse vocabulary words in sentences. For lower level students, limit the errors to one per sentence. Higher levels can handle multiple errors in one sentence, and you can increase the challenge by having one vocabulary error per sentence and one or more other errors, such as grammar or punctuation mistakes.

The activity itself is straightforward. Students will work in teams of 4-5 to correct the worksheet as quickly as possible. Each student makes one correction and passes the worksheet to the next person who makes the next correction. They continue to pass the worksheet around until it is complete. You can make it easier by allowing students to choose any remaining sentence to correct, or you can require them to work from top to bottom.

Teaching Tips:

To prevent one student from carrying the rest of the team, do not allow other team members to correct another correction. That is, a sentence cannot be corrected by a second student once someone has corrected it. This also prevents more assertive (but not necessarily more able) students from incorrectly correcting others' work.

Also, to keep things moving along you may want to have a time limit for each turn before students must pass the worksheet along.

Procedure:

1. In advance, prepare a worksheet with 10-15 sentences containing vocabulary errors.

2. Divide students into groups of 4-5. If possible, group the desks to facilitate easy passing of the worksheets.

3. Have students take turns making one correction and passing the worksheet to the next student to make one correction. They continue passing and correcting until the worksheet is complete.

4. When all teams are finished, go over the errors as a class. The team with the most correct sentences wins.

Dialogue Substitution

Skills: Reading/listening/speaking

Reading Sub-Skills: Reading out loud, predicting, inferring meaning from context

Time: 10-15 minutes

Level: Beginner

Materials Required: PowerPoint or handouts of photocopied textbook dialogue with parts removed.

Lower level textbooks contain many dialogues but their effectiveness is reduced when students don't have to listen to their partner in order to successfully complete their role. An easy solution to this is to provide the dialogues with key elements missing. In this case, you may want to remove key grammatical elements out of the conversation. For example, you could use this activity to work on subject-verb agreement if you leave the verb out. Or, you could leave the subject out as well.

Students then have to listen in order to respond appropriately. Dialogues are an excellent way for students to see how new grammar is used in real-life situations.

In terms of reading skills, there are a number of things this activity can help our students with. Perhaps most importantly, students have to use the context to infer meaning and figure out the appropriate word. They can also predict what will come next and work on reading out loud.

You may need to scaffold this activity by providing a list of possible grammar patterns that could be used to fill the gaps. Alternatively, you can make the activity more difficult or realistic by allowing students to complete the dialogue using any language that makes sense, even if it hasn't been presented in that lesson.

This activity is also useful for reviewing some basic conversation strategies: asking a speaker to repeat what he/she has said or asking for clarification (as well as others). This is an area where students may need a bit of scaffolding, such as a few ways to politely ask others to repeat themselves:

One more time, please?

Sorry, I didn't understand.

Also, remind students that when they speak to someone, they should be looking at the person, rather than at a handout or screen.

Teaching Tips:

29

This can work with any size class, but you may need to remind students to use their "inside voices." Also be sure to circulate around the class monitoring their language choices and making corrections as needed.

Procedure:

1. Before class, scan or photocopy a textbook dialogue with the target language (a grammatical point) removed.

2. Optionally, create a list of possible words or phrases that students can use to complete the dialogue or encourage students to use other words or phrases that will fit the target language. Also, introduce any language needed for practicing communication strategies (see above).

3. Divide students into pairs and have them take turns being A and B.

4.To extend the activity, have students change partners and repeat the dialogue, using different words to create a new conversation.

Find the Reference

Skill: Reading
Reading Sub-Skills: Identifying specific words/grammatical constructions, recognizing links
Time: 10+ minutes
Level: Beginner-intermediate
Materials Required: Newspaper article, pen

This is a noticing activity that helps students recognize links within a text. In newspaper writing, care is taken to avoid repetitive use of the subject's name. This is the opposite of most ESL material, which makes frequent use of repetition to reinforce language. Your students will read a newspaper article and circle all references to the subject in order to practice recognizing the subject even when various terms are used to reference it. For a completed example of this activity, please see: www.eslspeaking.org/reference.

Teaching Tip:

Use an actual newspaper, rather than a source such as *Breaking News English*, which may alter the text to reduce the use of varied referents.

Procedure:

1. Choose an article from a newspaper that has multiple references to the subject but uses a number of different referents such as, "Jones," "he," "him," "the 39-year-old," "the painter," "the father of two," etc.

2. Have the students read and circle each reference to the subject.

Flyer Time

Skills: Reading

Reading Sub-Skills: Scanning, inferring meaning from context, predicting

Time: 10+ minutes

Level: Beginner-intermediate

Materials Required: Prepared flyers/ads and questions

This activity is used to practice answering questions with a visual aid. This activity is designed to assist students with predicting and then scanning for specific information as well as inferring meaning from the context if the answer is not explicitly stated.

While your students are unlikely to be asked which bands are playing at X festival, they may need to answer questions about a presentation or report in English. In advance, prepare several event flyers or ads and questions. Prepare some questions that have the answers clearly stated:

"What time will _____ begin?"

"Where will this take place?"

Also include some questions that require the students to think about the event and use existing knowledge:

"Who do you think will be attending this event?"

31

"Will attendees need to do anything in advance?" (For example, make a reservation or buy tickets)

In class, give the flyer to your students and ask them to use it to answer your questions. Explain that not all of the answers are stated explicitly.

Procedure:

1. In advance, prepare several event flyers and questions (see above for examples) for your students to answer using the flyers.

2. Let your students know that not all questions are explicitly answered on the flyer.

3. Have your students use the flyer to answer the questions.

4. Ask the questions. Do not let your students read the answers word for word.

Identify This!

Skill: Reading

Reading Sub-Skills: Identifying words and grammatical constructions

Time: 5-10 minutes

Level: Beginner

Materials Required: A text

Beginners are often at the level where they are just beginning to understand the vocabulary words and basic grammatical constructions within a text. This activity can help them with this.

The way it works is that you can choose a certain thing that students have to look for. It may be as simple as finding all the numbers, colors, weather words, etc. Or, students may have to find verbs in the past tense. I generally choose this based on what I've been teaching my students in the past few lessons.

Procedure:

1. Choose a text with various examples of your target grammar or vocabulary.

2. Explain to students what they should be looking for (past tense verbs for example) and that they should circle each example they find.

3. Students compare answers with a partner

4. Check answers as a class.

5. This activity can easily lead into other reading exercises with the same text. Or, it could be a post-reading activity as well.

Puzzles

Skills: Reading/writing

Reading Sub-Skill: Reading for detail

Time: 10-30 minutes

Level: Beginner-intermediate

Materials Required: A puzzle

Puzzles are an excellent way to review vocabulary and I find that most students enjoy doing them, particularly teenagers. They can also work very well for "quiet" classes that don't have a lot of outgoing students in them where it's hard to do some of the more active games like charades. They help students read for detail as they have to pay close attention to exactly what the clue says in order to answer the question correctly.

It's really easy to make puzzles yourself using something like *Discovery.com*'s Puzzlemaker (www.discoveryeducation.com/free-puzzlemaker) and it's actually the preferable option since you can include all the specific vocabulary that you'd like. I prefer to use the criss-cross option because it has the most educational benefit since it deals with meanings as well as vocabulary words.

Teaching Tips:

It's up to you whether or not to allow dictionaries or textbooks. In my experience, dictionaries don't really help that much while the course book where the words came from really does. You could also say that for the first five minutes, they must only use their brains, but they can use anything they want after that. If there is a particularly hard one that no student is able to get, I'll give the entire class a hint.

Procedure:

1. Go to *Discovery.com* and find the Puzzlemaker.

2. Design your puzzle (criss-cross is best!), using words and definitions. Alternatively, you could give hints about the word related to the context you'd use it in instead of the actual definition. Here are two examples:

This animal has black and white stripes (skunk).

If a _____ sprays you, you'll smell really bad (skunk).

3. Have students complete the puzzle. I usually make it a bit competitive by putting them in pairs and awarding the first couple of teams a prize of some sort.

4. It's up to you whether or not to allow dictionaries or textbooks. In my experience, dictionaries don't really help that much while the course book where the words came from really does. You could also say that for the first five minutes, they must only use their brains, but they can use anything they want after that. If there is a particularly hard one that no student is able to get, I'll give the entire class a hint.

Reading Jigsaw

Skill: Reading

Reading Sub-Skills: Reading out loud, recognizing links, predicting

Time: 10 minutes

Level: High beginner

Materials Required: Jigsaw pieces with words written on them

This is a simple reading activity for high-beginner students which helps students with prediction and recognizing how a story fits together. The way it works is that you can write a story on the back sides of jigsaw puzzle pieces. It's more fun if all the pieces actually fit together. It depends on the level, but total beginners can work on sentences, while higher level beginners could work with a few sentences at once.

Then, students have to use a combination of how the pieces fit together, along with the words themselves to make the correct story. I like to have students do this in groups of 3-4 with a number of different puzzles which they can all rotate through. The teacher can check if the story is correct and also ask some simple comprehension questions to ensure that students are paying attention to what they're doing! Students can rotate through various stories.

Procedure:

1. In advance, write simple stories on the back of jigsaw puzzle pieces.

2. Put students into groups of 3-4 and have them complete each story.

3. The teacher can check to ensure the story is correct and ask some comprehension questions.

4. Students rotate through all the stories until they're done.

Rock-Scissors-Paper

Skills: Reading/speaking/listening

Reading Sub-Skills: Predicting, reading out loud

Time: 10-15 minutes

Level: Beginner

Materials Required: Matching strips of paper with questions + answers

Rock-Scissors-Paper is ideal to review key material right before a test. It works particularly well with questions and answers in the past tense. In terms of reading sub-skills, it helps students work on reading out loud as well as predicting what things they might hear in response to their corresponding question or answer.

The way it works is that you make up some questions and answers (matching) in a spreadsheet. Make enough so that each student can have five of them (total, not five questions *and* five answers). Repeating each question/answer pair a few times is fine for larger classes. Then print off a copy and cut out the paper strips.

In class, each student gets five strips of paper and then moves around the classroom trying to find their matches. When they find a match, they do rock-scissors-paper with their partner and the winner takes both strips of paper. The goal is to get as many matches as possible.

This game has the potential to become a little bit wild if you don't set up some ground rules at the start! Picture 20 students running around the classroom screaming in their native language. It's not ideal.

Here's how you can avoid this:

Make a rule about no shouting. Each student must talk 1:1 with another student (no groups or teams). If anyone is not following this rule, they will have to sit down until the activity is finished.

It's best to make matches that are not too similar to each other. They should be quite obvious because if not, you'll end up with all sorts of incorrect pairings at the end of the game (and students won't be able to find the correct matches because of this).

For example, things that are too similar:

What's your favourite game? I like soccer.

What's your favourite sport. I like to play soccer.

Better questions for this activity are:

What's your favourite board game? I like Monopoly.

What's your favourite sport to play? I like to play soccer.

Do you see what I mean? More specific questions are better than general ones.

At the end of the game, you can review some of the most important questions/answers that you want to highlight before your test, or that need to be emphasized before moving on to new material.

Quick tip: you can reuse these papers for other classes if you teach the same thing multiple times. Just get the papers back from the students at the end of the activity. However, this isn't always the case, so have a back-up plan in place if you can't!

Procedure:

1. Make up strips of paper with questions and answers (on separate papers). I usually do this by making up a grid of about 20 x 2. Then, write the corresponding questions/answers. Print out 1-5 copies (depending on the size of your class), cut the pieces out, and put them into a big envelope.

2. In class, give each student five random papers that are a mix of both questions and answers. They have to walk around the class finding their "match." They can do this by talking quietly with each other or reading the papers of the other person.

3. Once they find a match, they can rock-scissors-paper and the winner takes both papers.

The students with the most points at the end of the allotted time are the winners. Two papers (question/answer) count as one point.

4. Double-check the question/answer matches because sometimes students make mistakes. Emphasize to students that you will be checking their matches so they will try harder to make a correct match and not just randomly pair them up.

5. Bring a small prize for 2-3 of the winners.

Tic-Tac-Toe

Skills: Listening/speaking/reading

Reading Sub-Skill: Reading for detail

Time: 15 minutes

Level: Beginner-intermediate

Materials Required: Whiteboard

This is a review game for students to play in small groups. I usually make groups of four and then within the group, there are two opposing teams. Have students make a regular Tic-Tac-Toe board in their notebook or on some scrap paper.

Put up a list of review questions in a PowerPoint or give students a handout. Students must read for detail in order to be able to answer the question correctly. The teams take turns answering the questions and if correct, they get to mark a square on the grid with X or O and the first to get three in a row is the winner. The teacher can act as the referee in case of uncertainty about an answer.

Teaching Tip:

This game is over before it begins if your opponent doesn't know how to answer any questions or has never played Tic-Tac-Toe before. In order to prevent this, I put students in teams of two, trying to match a higher level student with a lower level one. Hopefully, at least one of the students will be able to answer questions and has some sort of Tic-Tac-Toe skill. If you know that many students will have a difficult time answering the questions, you can put some answer prompts up on the whiteboard or PowerPoint.

Procedure:

1. Put students in groups of four, two teams of two.

2. Students can make a normal Tic-Tac-Toe board on a piece of paper.

3. Put review questions in a PowerPoint, or give students a handout with them.

4. One person from each team does rock-scissors-paper to determine who will go first.

5. The first team has to answer the first question and if correct, gets to mark the board with either an X or O. The other team answers the next question and gets to mark one spot on the board if correct.

6. The first team to get three X's or O's in a row is the winner.

7. You can play numerous games and even have the "winners" move up and the "losers" move down like in King's Court until you have one final team that is the "King."

Word-Definition Match

Skills: Reading

Reading Sub-Skill: Scanning for key words in definitions that relate to the vocab word

Time: 5-10 minutes

Level: Beginner-intermediate

Materials Required: Cards or worksheet/whiteboard/PowerPoint

Card Version: Print one vocabulary word per card, and one definition on a separate card. You will need one set per student, pair or group and make sure to mix up the words and definitions before giving them to the students. How many words and definition matches are in a set depends on the level of the students but I find that at least eight pairs makes this activity challenging enough.

Worksheet/Whiteboard/PowerPoint Version: Create a word bank of current or review vocabulary and a list of definitions for students to draw a line (worksheet) or matching letters and numbers for whiteboard or PowerPoint.

39

Procedure (Card Version):

1. In advance, prepare cards with one word or definition per card. Print and laminate enough for each student, pair or group to have a set of at least eight matches. Mix up each set in random fashion before giving them to the students.

2. If you're having students work in pairs or small groups, divide the class accordingly and distribute a full set of cards to each. If students will be working alone, give each student a set of cards.

3. Have students match the words to their definitions as quickly as possible. Students can work on their scanning for key word skills as they compete to see who can finish first.

Procedure (Worksheet/Whiteboard/PowerPoint Version):

1. Have students match the words and definitions, by drawing a line (worksheet) or matching letters and numbers and writing their answers in their notebooks.

2. Have students trade papers to check.

ESL Reading Activities for Higher-Level Students

Activate Prior Knowledge

Skills: Speaking/reading

Reading Sub-Skill: Predicting content

Time: 5 minutes

Level: Intermediate-advanced

Materials Required: None

One of the most helpful things we can do for our students before they read something is to help activate their prior knowledge and set the context. An excellent way to do this for our higher-level students is to get them to talk about something before reading.

For example, maybe the text is a story about a vacation gone wrong. You can elicit some answers from students about bad things that can happen on vacation. For example:

- Getting robbed

- Missing a flight

- Losing a wallet or passport

- Getting sick

- Etc.

Then, have students talk with a partner for 2-3 minutes about if any of these things have happened to them. This helps them activate any prior knowledge they may have about vocabulary they could expect to read, as well as to personalize it. Both of these things will make for a richer, more valuable reading experience and can help bring some real life into the classroom.

This activity can lead into other reading exercises and activities.

Agony Aunt

Skills: Speaking/reading

Sub-Skills: Note-taking, reading for detail, inferring attitude/feeling

Time: 15-20 minutes

Level: Intermediate-advanced

Materials Required: Printed advice column questions and answers

This activity will get your students talking because everyone knows how to solve other people's problems! If your students are a bit more advanced, you can use actual advice columns. These can easily be found by searching on the Internet for "advice column" etc. The lower the students' level, the more you'll need to grade the language, or you can write your own advice column.

In terms of reading sub-skills, I like to get my students to take some notes as they're reading in order to work on their note-taking skills. It also helps with reading for detail and inferring the attitude or feeling of the person writing the letter.

I've done several variations of this activity and it has always been a hit. I begin with an introduction that shows a few advice column letters and answers. Discuss them a bit—most students will be familiar with the concept. Then, give your students a copy of a letter (not the same one from the introduction).

Version 1:

All the students receive the same letter. Each person has 3-8 minutes (depending on the level) to come up with some advice (separately). The class has a short discussion about what advice each person would give and why. You can also have students discuss their advice in small groups if you have a larger class.

Version 2:

All the students (small classes) or groups (big classes) receive a different letter. As above, each person/group is given time to read and think of some advice. You can begin the discussion time by having each person quickly summarize the problem they have read about, then give some advice and discuss that.

Teaching Tip:

If you are familiar with local celebrities popular with your students, you can use current gossip to spice up the lesson. If X pop star has just had a public breakup, write a letter from that person asking for help getting back together, finding a new boyfriend, etc. For the men, a rumor of a football star being traded works well to get advice on how to improve that player's game.

Procedure:

1. Show some level-appropriate advice column letters. Read them together and discuss.

Version 1:

1. All students get the same letter (not one from the introduction).

2. Each person has to read the letter and come up with some advice (separately).

3. Discuss each person's advice.

Version 2:

1. The students get different letters.

43

2. Give some time to read the letter and come up with some advice.

3. Discuss the problems and their advice.

Chapter Response

Skills: Speaking/writing

Reading Sub-Skills: Predicting, recognizing links, inferring attitude/feelings, understanding discourse markers

Time: 10-15 minutes

Level: Intermediate-advanced

Materials Required: None

Optional Materials: Printed list of questions

Chapter endings make handy stopping points to check your students' comprehension and build a bit of interest to keep up motivation for the next chapter. These questions can be answered orally as part of a book discussion or written in a reader response journal and then discussed in class.

Some questions you can ask include:

What surprised you in this chapter?

What feelings did you have as you read? What made you feel this way?

What words, phrases, or situations in the chapter would you like to have explained?

Would you recommend this novel to someone else? Why or why not?

How do the events in this story so far relate to your life?

Which character do you most relate to? In what way?

Which character most reminds you of someone in your life? In what way?

What do you hope to learn about (a character) as you continue reading?

What do you think will happen next?

What questions do you have that you hope will be answered in the next chapter?

I also like to include some questions related to discourse markers and how the text is organized. This can really help our students gain an awareness of the key differences among things they read. Finally, I also try to ask some very leading questions about links between various parts of the texts and how they connect to each other.

Procedure:

1. In advance, prepare a printed list of questions about the chapter.

2. Discuss together in class, or have the students write their answers for homework and you can discuss them in the next class.

Character Problems and Solutions

Skills: Reading/speaking/writing

Reading Sub-Skill: Inferring attitude/feeling/meaning

Time: 10-15 minutes

Level: Intermediate-advanced

Materials Required: None

This is a post-reading activity to include in a novel study or use with a short story. Choose a problem a character faced in the story. Discuss the problem and how the character solved it. Then, have your students brainstorm other ways the problem could have been dealt with. This is a sneaky grammar lesson. You can teach modals of regret (could/should/would have done/etc.) without getting too personal with your students.

In terms of reading sub-skills, it's heavy on inferring attitude, feelings and meaning. I also like to get my students to predict what could happen next if the text is unclear about it.

Procedure:

1. Choose a problem a character faced in the story.

2. Discuss the problem and how the character solved it.

3. Have your students brainstorm other ways the problem could have been dealt with.

Closest in Meaning

Skill: Reading

Reading Sub-Skills: Inferring meaning from context

Time: 10 minutes

Level: Intermediate-advanced

Materials Required: Sentences with corresponding match options

It's often the case when reading anything in a language that we're not fluent in to encounter words we don't know. Some people reach for their dictionary every single time this happens but this isn't necessary and it's certainly not efficient. Instead, a more effective way is to guess the meaning of the unknown word using context clues. This activity is designed to help our students with this important skill.

Make some sentences and for each one, have 2-3 corresponding sentences, one of which is obviously closest in meaning to the original than the other ones. I use a slightly higher level of vocabulary than the students are at and don't allow them to use their dictionaries. For example:

Focus: The professor delivered her lecture eloquently.

Answer: The professor's lesson was clear and easy to understand.

Extra Sentence 1: The professor's lecture was presented in a PowerPoint.

Extra Sentence 2: The professor's class was spoken too quickly.

You may want to have students work together in pairs to complete this activity, or at the very least, compare with a partner when they're done. After this, check answers together as a class.

Procedure:

1. In advance, write some sentences and some corresponding sentences. One should be closer in meaning to the original than the others and use some higher-level vocabulary throughout.

2. Students have to choose the sentence that is closest in meaning to the original using context clues, alone or in pairs.

3. If done alone, students can compare answers with a partner.

4. Check answers as a class and discuss helpful context clues used in the activity.

Cosmo Quiz

Skills: Speaking/listening/reading

Reading Sub-Skill: Reading for detail

Time: 10-20 minutes

Level: Intermediate-advanced

Materials Required: A *Cosmo* quiz or *Cosmo*-type quiz

If you are a guy, you may not be familiar with the quiz in each month's edition of *Cosmopolitan* magazine. These generally predict something about your relationship style, finances, etc. In other words, they are quiz-style horoscopes. They are pretty fun to do as a group, because they are not meant to be taken seriously, but can tell you a little something about the quiz-taker. The best part is that this activity helps students with reading for detail as they have to carefully choose which answer applies to them.

Prep could not be easier. Simply find a few old issues of *Cosmo* and copy the quizzes.

You may want to go over vocabulary as a pre-reading part of the lesson. Also, some of them are a bit risqué, so decide for yourself if you want to edit them a bit. I've had all-female classes and kept it a little racy, but all the students were about my age. If you're unsure about whether it's a good idea or not to use racy content, imagine your boss observing the class—if they'd be unhappy about it, choose something else.

In class, begin with a brief discussion of personality quizzes: has anyone ever taken one, etc. Divide students into pairs or small groups of 3-4 and give them one or two quizzes with the results on a different page. Have them read the questions and discuss the answers, keeping track of their answers, if they want. You can wrap up with a survey of results and questions of how students feel about the quizzes. Are they accurate, fun, or a waste of time?

Teaching Tips:

You can find quizzes on their website: http://www.cosmopolitan.com/content/quizzes/, but the questions are given one at a time, so if you can get your hands on print quizzes, it will make your life easier.

If you think they are inappropriate for your class, you can always just make up a quiz in the same *Cosmo* style: ten multiple choice personality questions with points assigned to each answer. There are usually results for three point ranges.

You can either give everyone one quiz and each group reads and answers the questions together, or you can have students alternate asking and answering. You can extend the activity by having students change partners and taking a different quiz.

Procedure:

1. In advance, gather several different issues of *Cosmo* magazine and copy the quizzes. You may need to edit the questions or leave some out.

2. Begin class by asking if anyone has ever taken a personality quiz and how they feel about them.

3. Divide students into pairs or small groups of 3-4 and give them one or two quizzes with the results on a separate page.

4. Have them read the questions and discuss the answers, keeping track of their answers, if they want.

5. Optionally, extend the activity by having groups change partners and take a new quiz.

Extensive Reading

Skill: Reading

Reading Sub-Skill: Reading fluency

Time: Variable

Level: Intermediate-advanced

Materials Required: Graded readers or novels

It's often the case that students have to read for detail, but reading just for fun in English is not something that they often do. That's why I like to include some extensive reading in my classes whenever it's practical.

By practical, I mean that I have access to a small library of graded readers or English novels at an appropriate reading level. Or, a budget to purchase this. And the other factor to consider is the amount of class time you have each week. If only an hour, then it may not be enough time to consider doing this. However, if you have 3+ hours, spending 20-30 minutes each week on extensive reading can be a great use of class time.

The key is that students choose something to read that's slightly before their level. Then, they can just read it easily without having to worry about stopping every minute or two to look up a word. I emphasize to my students that the goal is to work on reading fluency and to put away their dictionary and just read for fun.

Procedure:

1. Students choose something to read at a level slightly below where they're at.

2. Read for 10-15 minutes. The beginning or end of each class works well.

3. Students keep track of the book and page number to continue with the same book next class.

Headline Prediction Practice

Skill: Reading

Reading Sub-Skill: Predicting content

Time: 5-10 minutes

Level: Intermediate-advanced

Materials Required: Text with a headline

One way to improve reading skills is to have in mind what we're about to read. This primes our brains to receive information and by doing this, reading comprehension is generally better. It's also helpful to have some key vocabulary words in mind. Furthermore, do a modeling of asking the 5Ws + H (who, what, where, when, why and how) about key words in a sample title with intermediate students, and with advanced (depending on the class) give a brief reminder to use those questions when predicting

To do this with students, choose a story that has an interesting headline that is somewhat vague and could have many possible outcomes or reasons. Then, in pairs, students talk with their partner about what they think might happen. Elicit some answers from the students but don't give away too much! Write on the whiteboard or in a PPT slide 3-4 different ideas that the students have.

Hand out the text for the students to read and they can quickly read through it to see which of their predictions was correct, if any. This can lead into a more detailed second reading activity.

Procedure:

1. Show students an interesting headline.

2. In pairs, students predict what might happen, or what the cause of the problem is.

3. Elicit some answers and write 3-4 of them on the board.

4. Students quickly read the text to see if any of their guesses were correct.

Paraphrasing and Summarizing Practice

Skills: Reading/writing

Reading Sub-Skill: Paraphrasing, summarizing

Time: Variable

Level: Intermediate-advanced

Materials Required: Passage to paraphrase (lecture, newspaper article, etc.)

Paraphrasing and summarizing are important writing skills and there is certainly some overlap between the two. If your students are planning to take a test such as the TOEFL, TOEIC, or IELTS, they will need to be able to do these things effectively. What's the difference? Paraphrasing is expressing the meaning of something using different words with the goal to achieve greater clarity. Summarizing is giving an overview of the main points of something. This activity focuses specially on the former sub-skill.

To help your students practice paraphrasing, choose a short newspaper article. They can begin by circling words which cannot be changed: places, names, dates, etc. Then, they can see if any information can be combined or rearranged. Next, they could consider the best synonyms to replace the nouns, verbs, and adjectives. Finally, they can reread the original text and compare it with your paraphrase. Do both texts have the same meaning? If not, keep trying.

Many students think that summarizing a text is extremely difficult but it's possible to work on this skill with them. You may want to do a warm-up exercise by choosing a popular movie that students have seen. Ask them to summarize the story in one sentence. If you're working with intermediate students, consider putting a fill in the blank summary sentence on the board to help them. Once they realize they already do summaries in their day to day lives, they'll have more confidence that they can do the 'academic' style too.

Teaching Tip:

For advanced students, it may be possible to have them do both summarizing and paraphrasing together. However, for intermediate students it's important to only ask them to do one of the two, and later if they've mastered each, try doing both of them in the same activity.

Procedure for Paraphrasing:

1. Give students a passage that they can read.

2. Students decide which words can't be changed and are most important.

3. Students decide which information can be combined or rearranged, as well as think of some alternative synonyms to use.

4. Students prepare their final paraphrase draft and then compare with another student or hand it in to the teacher.

Procedure for Summarizing:

1. Choose a movie or something that most students are familiar with that has a story element to it.

2. Ask them to summarize the story in one sentence, working together with a partner.

3. Elicit some answers from the class and discuss which ones are most accurate.

Think about the Characters More Deeply

Skills: Reading/speaking/writing

Reading Sub-Skills: Reading for detail, inferring attitude/feeling/meaning, identifying the text type/purpose/organization

Time: 15+ minutes

Level: Intermediate-advanced

Materials Required: Fiction reading

When reading fiction, here are some ideas to help students think about the characters more deeply which will help them understand the overall text.

- Make a fact file about the main character. Here are some things to include in this section. How old is the character? Who is in their family? What is their job?

- Compare and contrast two main characters in the story. How are they the same? How are they different?

- Usually, the main character in a story changes in some way by the end. How did the main character in the story you have just read change in their actions or thinking? How were they at the beginning? What was different at the end? What caused them to change?

- Consider one scene from a different character's point of view. In English, we say every fight has three sides: your version, my version, and the truth. This is because all of us see the same event in different ways.

- Think of a situation that is not in the book. What would the main character do in that situation? Why do you think so?

Think about the Plot More Carefully

Skills: Reading/writing/speaking

Reading Sub-Skills: Inferring attitude/feeling/meaning, reading for detail, identifying the text type/organization

Time: 15+ minutes

Level: Intermediate-advanced

Materials Required: Fiction reading

If you teach novels or short stories in your classes, then you could consider doing this activity. Thinking about the plot more carefully will also improve your reading comprehension skills. Here are some ideas to help our students consider the storyline more deeply.

- Make a timeline of important events in the story. How does one event lead to another?

- Where does the action occur? Make a list of important locations in the story. Would the story be the same in any location? Why or why not?

- When you read a book in English, write a review on *Goodreads* or *Amazon*. Let the world know what you thought of the book.

- Make a summary of what you read in 3-4 sentences (either writing or speaking out loud to yourself).

- Pretend you are the character in the story. Write a postcard from a certain point in time to another character.

- Draw a map of the book's setting.

- Create a poem about a book or story character.

- Write a diary entry as if you were a person in the story.

Use Context Clues

Skill: Reading

Reading Sub-Skill: Inferring meaning from context

Time: 10+ minutes

Level: Intermediate-advanced

Materials Required: Story or novel

This activity helps students develop their ability to use context clues when reading. Simply have them write down five words they do not know as they are reading. Have them note the page number and paragraph for easy reference. Once they have finished reading, have them find those words again and write down the sentence it is used in as well as the sentence before and after it.

Instruct students to note if there is a prefix or suffix, and what part of speech the unknown word might belong to. Next, write down the word that is before the unknown word, and the word after it. Ask them if those help to infer the meaning of the unknown word. After that, write down 2-3 words before, and 2-3 words after, the unknown word (if there are any) to see if those help. Lastly, write down the sentence before, and the sentence after, the unknown word sentence.

Once they have written these sentences, have them use the sentences to guess the meaning of each unknown word and write that as well. Finally, have them compare their guess to the dictionary definition. Are they close? If not, was the word used in an ambiguous way, or could they have made better use of context clues?

Teaching Tip:

Once students are familiar with this activity, consider relegating it to homework.

Procedure:

1. As an addition to a regular reading activity, have your students make note of five words in the story they do not know.

55

2. Have them make note of each word, the page number, and the paragraph number and continue reading.

3. Once they have finished reading, have them go back and find those words again and write down the sentence it is used in as well as the sentence before and after it.

4. Then, have them use the sentences to guess the meaning of each unknown word and write that as well.

5. Have them compare their guesses with the dictionary definitions of each word.

What's the Main Idea?

Skill: Reading

Reading Sub-Skills: Summarizing, note-taking

Time: 10-20 minutes (depends on the length of the text)

Level: Intermediate-advanced

Materials Required: A text

An important reading sub-skill is the ability to pick out the key points and summarize. This is important in real life for things like reading reports or preparing for a test, but also for English reading proficiency exams. This simple activity is designed to practice this skill.

Give students a text appropriate to their level. More advanced students can handle longer ones. Ask students to read through it carefully, taking notes as they do this about the main points. Or, they may wish to circle or highlight key words.

Then, students have to summarize the main idea of the article in 1-3 sentences. How many sentences depends on the length of the text. Next, they can compare with a partner and finally, the class can discuss some of the answers together.

I generally have an "ideal" summary for students to compare theirs to but of course, there are many different versions possible. The main thing is that students are able to communicate the main idea or points of the text. However, by showing a summary it's possible to set a standard for testing and grading that students can use to compare their own to and get an idea of what they need to practice and improve upon.

Procedure:

1. Choose an appropriate text.

2. Students read the text, taking notes or circling key words.

3. Students summarize it in 1-3 sentences and compare with a partner.

4. Discuss together as a class.

7 Step ESL Reading Lesson Plan

There are a few distinct steps to follow when teaching reading skills. Although the reading passage changes, the steps do not! First of all, be clear about the objectives of the lesson. That is, what is the lesson trying to achieve and what will success for the students look like?

Step #1: Set the Context

Context is everything when learning a language. Without it, students are just learning random bits of grammar and vocabulary but they don't have a way to put it together into a cohesive system within their brains.

To start a lesson off, do this 100% of the time. A great teacher never forgets this! And of course, the context for each lesson will change from day to day so don't use the same old stale thing, okay?

ALWAYS help students by providing as much context as possible by activating prior knowledge. An easy way to do this in a reading or listening lesson is have students talk together for a couple minutes about something. During the CELTA course, I had this story about a man who was living in an airport. I was lucky, perhaps, in that it was something that the students were really interested in! In order to set the context, I had students talk about five things that people do when they have to wait in the airport for a long time (sleep/watch TV/eat + drink, etc.).

Step #2: Pre-Reading Task

This is where you have students do something related to the reading. You can teach/have students review some of the key vocabulary in the passage, or do something like a prediction task.

In the case I mentioned previously, I told my students that they were going to read a story about a guy who lived in an airport for 17 years. And that he only left eventually because he got sick and had to go to the hospital. The students had to guess why they think he stayed there so long.

I elicited five answers and wrote them on the board to lead into step #3, making sure that one of the answers was the correct one.

Step #3: Gist Reading Task

You should always have students read for gist. This is because it gets them out of the extremely bad habit they often have of reading every single word in excruciating detail. When people read in their first language, they never read all the words. Instead, they just skim or scan the page to look for the information they need.

You need to help your students get practice doing this in English. It's also useful if they're doing any sort of English examinations because they often contain quite long reading passages which students have to digest in a limited amount of time. It can really help them if you teach them how to read and only look for specific information.

For the airport example, I gave students only two minutes and they had to quickly skim through the passage to find out why the man stayed in the airport for so long. Always have students compare answers with each other and then check as a class. But, this is a gist reading task so give the correct answer but do NOT go into any sort of depth. Students will have another chance in the next task to catch all the nuances of the passage.

Step #4: Main Reading Task

This is where students take a more detailed look at the reading and can read more slowly and carefully. You can give them some short answer, True/False questions, etc. However, at this stage I try to break students of another bad habit: always looking at their cell-phone dictionaries. I tell them that they can use it only one time, but otherwise they can just guess and use the surrounding context to give them some clues.

Students compare answers with a partner or small group and then you can check together as a class. You can go into a bit more depth with explanations at this stage if necessary. You could also work on some pronunciation at this time if there are any problem words.

Step #5: Application

In this ESL lesson plan stage, students take the ideas and go a bit deeper with them. For the airport example, I had students work together with a partner to think of five interesting questions that they'd ask the man if they had the chance to meet him in person.

After that, I had one person pretend to be a journalist while the other one had to be the man in the airport. The journalist conducted an interview and made sure to ask a few follow-up questions as well. I finished off the lesson by talking about what eventually happened to the man (I looked it up on the Internet).

Step #6: Homework (Optional)

You may wish to assign some homework to your students as a way to follow-up. Or, add some optional worksheets to your online tool for students to use if they'd like to.

Step #7: Post-Reading Activities

You may wish to include some post-reading activities into your classes. These can extend an hour long class into a two-hour one for example. Or, you may wish to do it over two classes. Some of the things you can do with your students are to have them think more deeply about the characters or plot.

Or, you may want them to:

- Find examples of a certain part of speech
- Search for examples of a certain grammar point
- Look for metaphors and similes

- Do some worksheets

- Watch some videos about the same topic

- Listen to some related songs

- Something fun (get creative!)

- Do some kind of writing activity

- Etc.

Reading Lesson Plan FAQs

There are a number of important questions that people have about planning reading lessons. Here are the answers to some of the most common ones.

Does this Style of Reading Class Work for Any Level of Student?

That's another great question! This template assumes that your students have a basic level of English reading and are able to do things like compare answers with their partner. It's best for at least high beginners, and then can work on through up to advanced level students.

For students who are struggling with basic reading skill or vocabulary, you'll want to focus on that first before worrying too much about comprehension.

Can I Use this ESL Lesson Plan Template for Children?

This style of lesson works better for high school students or adults than it does younger children. It assumes that students are able to do things like compare answers with a partner, or have a short discussion for a lead-in or warm-up. Younger kids are often not at the maturity and attention level to be able to handle this.

Topic Ideas for ESL Reading Lessons

This reading lesson plan sample lends itself well to just about any topic under the sun.

Seriously, the sky is the limit. However, here are a few things to keep in mind when planning an ESL reading lesson plan.

Choose Timeless Topics

If I'm going to put the time and effort into planning an ESL reading lesson, then I want to be able to use it again in the future. This means that I choose timeless, or evergreen topics that are of interest to a wide group of people and ages. If I do this, I'll have plenty of opportunities to recycle the lesson in the future.

Social Science usually has a wealth of good stories, material and topics that lead to a great conversation. Once you plan a few of these reading lessons, you'll have a variety of go-to lessons you can pull together very quickly.

Use *Google Drive*

In order to recycle your reading lesson plans effectively, use *Google Drive*. You can go in there, make a few quick changes and have your "new" lesson ready to go in just a few minutes.

Base your Lesson Plan on an Article

Of course, a *reading lesson* should be based on an article of some kind. This is obvious, but it's worth noting. You can find them online, or in textbooks.

Don't be Afraid to Adapt the Language

If you want to talk about a certain topic, but can't find an appropriate article, don't be afraid to take one and adapt the language. I usually do the following:

- Shorten the article

- Remove complicated vocabulary and terms

- Take out complicated grammatical constructions or parts of speech

Keep the Reading Short

Unless you have a class that is 3-4 hours long, you'll want to keep the reading reasonably short. In general, it shouldn't take students more than 1/5 of the class time to read the article. Sure, you can assign it for homework, but many students won't complete it so I like to give class time for this.

English Reading Test-Taking Tips

When my students ask me advice about improving their scores on English proficiency tests, here's what I tell them.

Whether you are taking the TOEFL, TOEIC, IELTS, or some other test with a reading component, there are a few things you should do to read for a test.

1. Read the questions first. This is a test with a time limit. You are not trying to understand everything; you are trying to answer as many questions correctly as possible within that time limit. By reading the questions, you will know what to look for in the text. Do NOT read the answer (choices) section, as this will just confuse you and waste time.

2. Figure out what type of question it is. Will you be looking for context clues for a definition, synonym, or antonym? Cause and effect relationship? The author's purpose (entertainment, information, persuasion, etc.)? The main idea and/or details? A timeline or sequence of events? A character analysis (for example, how did the character feel in paragraph 4?)?

All About Keywords for English Reading Comprehension Tests

1. Circle the key words if you are allowed to write on the test paper. If you are not allowed to, write them on a sheet of scrap paper. These are the numbers, nouns, 5W and H words, etc. that tell you what information you need to find.

2. Scan the text looking for those keywords, synonyms, or (in the case of 5W and H words) transition words which match the words you have circled. For example, if one question begins with "why", you should look for words and phrases like: because, for the reason that, so, as a

result, etc.

3. Underline those keywords in the text (if you can write on the test booklet) and reread the question you think it might answer. Now, carefully reread the sentence with underlined words. Most texts on timed tests will have the answer in the sentence with the keywords. If not, almost all of the rest will have the answer in the sentence before or after the sentence with the keywords. Only a few will require you to keep reading.

4. Once you have found the answer to the question in the text, read all of the possible answers following the question. Choose the answer which best answers the question.

NEVER do This!

No matter what, do not spend too much time on one passage or one question. When you do reading tests, you're often under a time crunch. There is a lot to read, and plenty of questions to answer in a short time. If you don't understand something, spend a little bit of time trying to figure it out, but not too much. Go on to the next reading passage, or set of questions.

Come back to it at the end if you have time. Don't get stuck on any one thing and not finish a lot of the test because of it.

Advanced Level English Reading Test-Taking Tips

If you are an advanced level student and want some pro tips for English reading tests, here is the section for you!

1. There may be more than one good answer for English reading tests, but one will be best.

2. Other answers are distractors—they seem correct, if you are reading quickly, but one detail in the answer makes it incorrect.

3. Watch out for answers which include a direct quote from the text, but are unrelated to the question.

4. If you are not sure which answer is best, cross out the ones you know are wrong. Then, you won't have to remind yourself again.

5. Watch out for other tricks, such as the question giving you one paragraph, but additional correct information is in another paragraph. The correct answer will only include information from the paragraph named in the question.

Always Follow the Instructions for English Reading Exams

Follow the instructions! This seems obvious, but you may be worried about finding the answers and don't notice the instructions. On the IELTS, the reading portion has written answers.

If you do any of the following, your answer will be incorrect, even if it is really correct:

- misspell your answer

- use incorrect grammar

- make other mistakes, such as: writing an answer which is too long, choosing one answer but you should choose two, answering "true" to a Yes/ No question

Before You Go

If you found these ESL reading activities useful, please head on over to *Amazon* and leave a review. It will help other teachers like you find the book. Also be sure to check out my other books on *Amazon* at www.amazon.com/author/jackiebolen.

If you can't get enough ESL games, activities and other useful stuff for the classroom in this book, you can get even more goodness delivered straight to your inbox every week. I promise to respect your privacy—your name and email address will never be shared with anyone for any reason. Sign-up here.

Made in the USA
Columbia, SC
08 September 2023

22601476R00040